THE LAWYERS OF DICKENS
AND THEIR CLERKS

BY

ROBERT D. NEELY
of the Omaha Bar

THE LAWBOOK EXCHANGE, LTD.
Clark, New Jersey

ISBN 978-1-58477-091-6

Lawbook Exchange edition 2002, 2018

The quality of this reprint is equivalent to the quality of the original work.

THE LAWBOOK EXCHANGE, LTD.
33 Terminal Avenue
Clark, New Jersey 07066-1321

*Please see our website for a selection of our other publications
and fine facsimile reprints of classic works of legal history:*
www.lawbookexchange.com

Library of Congress Cataloging-in-Publication Data

Neely, Robert D. (Robert Donald), b. 1887.
    The lawyers of Dickens and their clerks / by Robert D. Neely.
      p. cm.
    Originally published: Boston: Christopher Pub. House, 1938.
    ISBN 1-58477-091-0 (alk. paper)
      1. Dickens, Charles, 1812-1870--Characters--Lawyers. 2. Dickens,
Charles, 1812-1870--Knowledge--Law. 3. Law and literature--History--19th
century. 4. Lawyers in literature. I. Title.

PR4589 .N46 2000
823'.8--dc21

                      00-021520

Printed in the United States of America on acid-free paper

THE LAWYERS OF DICKENS
AND THEIR CLERKS

BY

ROBERT D. NEELY
of the Omaha Bar

The Christopher Publishing House
Boston, U. S. A.

PRINTED IN THE UNITED STATES OF AMERICA

The Lawyers of Dickens
and Their Clerks

*"We lawyers are always curious, always inquisitive, always picking up odds and ends for our patchwork minds, since there is no knowing when and where they may fit into some corner."—
Little Dorrit.*

Charles J. H. Dickens was born at Portsea the seventh day of February, 1812. When less than a month old he was baptized at St. Mary's Kingston, the village church of Portsea. His schooling was rather limited, inasmuch as he did not attend until he was nine years of age and was obliged to leave seven years later. At the age of fifteen the little boy passed to the status of an attorney's clerk—what would now be called an office boy. He was in the office of Charles Molloy, an attorney of Symond's Inn and afterwards with the firm of Ellis and Blackmore of 1 Raymonds Building, Gray's Inn. He later became a reporter in the Doctors' Commons, which was the dwelling place of the proctors and advocates whose practise lay in the Ecclesiastical, Admiralty and Prize Courts.

It has been said that he began life as a lawyer, got tired of the dull routine and turned to literature. As a matter of fact he never had a chance to become a prac-

7

tising lawyer for the very good reason that he did not have the necessary financial backing. In his day the applicant for admission to the bar was obliged, either to register as a student at one of the Inns of Court, or become an articled clerk. An advance of 100 pounds was required as a condition precedent to registration for the three years of study which was necessary before the candidate was qualified to be called to the bar. A substantial payment was also needed when the prospective barrister sought entrance into the legal profession by the route of an articled clerk. Both roads were closed to Dickens. He worked to earn a livelihood and apparently had no intention of becoming an active practitioner. After quitting his clerical job, he was employed by a newspaper. Because of his proficiency as a shorthand reporter, he was assigned to the difficult task of reporting proceedings in Parliament.

Dickens' father was employed as a clerk in the Navy Pay office from 1815 to 1825 when he was dismissed on account of a retrenchment program. He then went into newspaper work. He became involved in financial difficulties when Charles was a small boy and was obliged to serve a term in prison for debt. As Sam Weller put it, "He run a match agin the Constable and vun it." In those days, if a judgment was unpaid, a body execution could be obtained and the debtor jailed. The character of J. Wilkins Micawber—that impecunious, improvident man, who shifted from one position to another, and was always waiting for something to turn up—was modeled in part after the author's father. Dickens spent some of his time in prison during his father's confinement and that experience evidently made a lasting impression on his mind.

As a result of his clerical and reporting work, Dickens became familiar with the routine of a law office. He was obliged to visit courts of law of all types, to serve subpoenas and copy writs, to prepare statements of fact and copy folio after folio of lengthy documents, such as briefs and pleadings. Later on in his career, he was plaintiff in five Chancery suits against certain publishers who had pirated Christmas Carol. Thomas Noon Talfourd, a well-known lawyer of that day, and author of the first Copyright Act, acted as one of his counsel in the copyright suits and revised the trial scene in Pickwick Papers for him. It is not surprising therefore that Dickens should have employed his wonderful powers of observation on the pageant of the law.

One of his most marked prejudices was his dislike of lawyers and all that pertained to the machinery of government. He firmly believed the sentiment which he so adroitly expressed in Nicholas Nickleby:

"There are many pleasant fictions of the law in constant operation, but there is not one so pleasant or practically humorous as that which supposes every man to be of equal value in its impartial eye, and the benefits of all laws to be equally attainable, by all men, without the smallest reference to the furniture of their pockets."

His contact with the legal profession and the courts evidently engendered in him an intense hatred for the whole bar—few of his lawyers are any credit to the profession. Speaking about them through the lips of David Copperfield, he says:

"I despised them, to a man. Frozen-out old gardeners in the flower-beds of the heart, I took a personal offence against them all. The Bench was nothing to me but an insensible blunderer. The Bar had no more tenderness or poetry in it, than the bar of a public house."

Despite the fact—some of the caustic critics of today would probably say because of the fact—that most of his lawyers are rascals, his character sketches are remarkably true to life. Served by all manner of clerks, these legal gentlemen afford a fascinating study for lawyers and laymen alike.

In Pickwick Papers, Dickens effectively describes the different classes of law clerks:

"Scattered about in various holes and corners of the Temple are certain dark and dirty chambers, in and out of which, all morning in vacation, and half the evening too in term time, there may be seen constantly hurrying, with bundles of papers under their arms, and protruding from their pockets, an almost uninterrupted succession of lawyers' clerks. There are several grades of lawyers' clerks. There is the articled clerk, who has paid a premium, and is an attorney in perspective, who runs a tailor's bill, receives invitations to parties, knows a family in Gower Street, and another in Tavistock Square: who goes out of town every long vacation to see his father, who keeps live horses innumerable; and who

JAGGERS

is, in short, the very aristocrat of clerks. There is
the salaried clerk—out of door, or indoor, as the
case may be— who devotes the major part of his
thirty shillings a week to his personal pleasure and
adornment, repairs half-price to the Adelphi Theater
at least three times a week, dissipates majestically at
the cider cellars afterwards, and is a dirty caricature of the fashion which expired six months ago.
There is the middle-aged copying clerk, with a large
family, who is always shabby, and often drunk. And
there are the office lads in their first surtouts, who
feel a befitting contempt for boys at day-schools,
club as they go home at night for saveloys and porter,
and think there's nothing like 'life.' "

Guppy, Wemmick, Swiveller and other skillfully
drawn representatives of this important part of the
English legal system are paraded before the eyes of the
reader.

One of the most impressive barristers introduced by
Charles Dickens is Jaggers, the central figure in Great
Expectations. Here is a great criminal lawyer, in large
practice at the Old Bailey, whose services were sought
by all involved in the toils of the law, confident that to
have Jaggers on your side meant ultimate, if not
instantaneous, freedom.

"He was a burly man of an exceedingly dark
complexion, with an exceedingly large head and a
corresponding large hand. *   *   * He was pre-
maturely bald on the top of his head, and had bushy
black eyebrows that wouldn't lie down, but stood up
bristling. His eyes were set very deep in his head,
and were disagreeably sharp and suspicious. He had

a large watch chain, and strong black dots where his
beard and whiskers would have been if he had let
them. * * *. Mr. Jaggers never laughed; but he
wore great bright, creaking boots, and in poising
himself on those boots, with his large head bent down
and his eyebrows joined together, awaiting an
answer, he sometimes caused the boots to creak, as
if *they* laughed in a dry and suspicious way. * * *.
If anybody, of whatsoever degree, said a word that
he didn't approve of, he instantly required to have
it 'taken down.' If anybody wouldn't make an admission, he said, 'I'll have it out of you!' and if anybody made an admission, he said, 'Now I have got
you!' The magistrates shivered under a single bite
of his finger. Thieves and thief-takers hung in dread
rapture on his words, and shrank when a hair of his
eyebrows turned in their direction. * * *

"He always carried a pocket handkerchief of rich
silk and of imposing proportions, which was of great
value to him in his profession. I have seen him so
terrify a client or a witness by ceremoniously unfold-
ing his pocket handkerchief, as if he were immediately
going to blow his nose, and then pausing, as if he
knew he would not have time to do it, before such
client or witness committed himself, that the self-
committal has followed directly, quite as a matter of
course."

As his confidential clerk Wemmick told Pip, narrator
and hero of the story, in relating how Jaggers had
secured the acquittal of Molly, Estella's mother, from a
murder charge, "To sum up, Sir, Mr. Jaggers was
altogether too many for the jury and they gave in."
The prosecution had charged this woman with the
murder of a rival for the affections of her paramour,
Abel Magwitch, Pip's unknown benefactor. The mur-

dered woman was very much larger and stronger than
the accused. She was found dead in a barn, bruised,
scratched and torn and had evidently been held by the
throat and choked at the last. At the trial Jaggers
presented his client with sleeves so skillfully contrived
that her arms had a delicate look. The back of her
hands were lacerated and the question was whether
the cuts came from finger nails. Jaggers showed that
she had struggled through a lot of brambles not as high
as her face but which she could not have got through
and kept her hands out. And bits of those brambles
were actually found in her skin and put in evidence.
The brambles in question were found on examination
to have been broken through and even had little shreds
of her dress and little spots of blood upon them here
and there. What jury could withstand this evidence
when analyzed for them by Jaggers with all the force
of his compelling personality.

When this unfortunate woman went to work for
Jaggers after her acquittal, with her mind somewhat
impaired at intervals, he dominated her completely and
she never left his service. On the occasion of Pip's
dining with Jaggers, the host took occasion to compel
the woman to display her scarred wrists to the company.
"There's power here," he said, tracing the sinews in
her forearm with his forefinger. "Very few men have
the power of wrist that this woman has." How proud
he was of his ability to gain his end—transform brute
strength into fragility by the arrangement of a sleeve
and wrest verdicts from juries by sheer force of person-

ality.   How many times have modern barristers prac-
ticed similar duplicity to gain their end.

The dominating force of this man Jaggers is most
effectively demonstrated when he makes his appearance
at the Inn of the Three Jolly Bargemen to advise Pip
that he has "great expectations."   A highly popular
murder had been committed and Mr. Wopsle, parish
clerk and leading citizen of the village, "who had a
deep voice which he was uncommonly proud of," was
reading the newspaper account of the crime aloud to an
assembled group, with great elocutionary flourish.
Wopsle declaimed with all the gestures and vocal
accomplishments of a Shakespearian actor, and at the
conclusion of the performance everybody quickly agreed
that it was a case of wilful murder.   Jaggers, loitering
nearby, had heard and seen the whole performance.
With an expression of contempt on his face, and biting
the side of his great forefinger as he habitually did, he
proceeded to question Wopsle, in a blustering and in-
solent manner, as to his knowledge of the law of England:

> "Do you know, or do you not know, that the law
> of England supposes every man to be innocent until
> he is proved—proved—to be guilty?   Do you know
> that none of these witnesses have been cross-
> examined?   Does not the newspaper account dis-
> tinctly state that the prisoner expressly said that his
> legal advisers had instructed him altogether to
> reserve his defence?"

Wopsle was quickly put to rout by the questions propounded to him by this intruding stranger with the big

head and penetrating eyes. It was clear to everyone
that a mistake had been made in concluding that murder
had been committed.

Pip was an orphan who lived with his sister. When
he was a small boy he befriended an escaped convict he
chanced to find hiding on the moor. The man demanded
that Pip bring him a file and some food. The boy ran to
his sister's house and returned with the articles. The convict was Abel Magwitch, father of Estella, with whom
Pip subsequently fell desparately in love. Although
Magwitch was recaptured and returned to prison, he
was later expatriated and made a fortune while living
abroad. Pip evidently reminded him of his small
daughter who he thought had been killed in infancy by
his mistress. Magwitch appointed Jaggers as Pip's
guardian and supplied him with sufficient money to
enable Pip to live in luxury for many years. In the
meantime Estella had been placed in the care of Miss
Havisham, a wealthy woman, whose intended husband
had failed to put in his appearance at the hour fixed for
their wedding. Because of that experience, Miss Havisham became a recluse. She adopted Estella and trained
her to be a heartless flirt. As a small boy, Pip was taken
to Miss Havisham's house frequently. There he met
Estella, and as he grew older, lost his heart to her.

During all the years following the announcement by
Jaggers that he had great expectations, Pip was satisfied
in his own mind that Miss Havisham was supplying
him with money and that strange lady made no effort to
correct that impression, notwithstanding she had full

knowledge of it. Pip did not know that Magwitch was his patron until the convict returned to England some years later and revealed the secret. Under the law of England as it existed at that time, an exiled person was forbidden to return under penalty of death. Compeyson, companion in crime of Magwitch and his bitter enemy, learned that the latter was in England and notified the authorities. Although Pip made every effort to get him out of the country, Magwitch was apprehended and returned to prison. He died there before the death sentence could be imposed and his estate was forfeited to the crown. Thus were Pip's "great expectations" dispelled and he was left in poverty.

When Pip went to London for the first time after he had been advised of his good fortune he called, as he had been directed to do, at Jaggers' office to make the necessary arrangements with his guardian. He was greatly impressed by what he saw and heard there. A large number of people were waiting for Jaggers to return from court. Pip particularly noticed an excitable Jew endeavoring to make arrangements with Wemmick, the lawyer's clerk, to retain Jaggers. When he found that the lawyer was already engaged by the opposition, he offered, without effect, unlimited sums in an effort to induce him to abandon his contract of employment. In another group Pip heard someone say:

"Jaggers is for him, Melia, and what *more* can you have?"

As soon as Jaggers came into view, there was a rush for him. The lawyer's first question was always whether Wemmick had been paid. Upon receiving assurances that the necessary retainer had been deposited, Jaggers immediately ordered all of them away. In one instance he indicated that he would have Wemmick return the client's money unless they left at once. This threat had the desired effect and the people departed forthwith.

When Pip dined with Jaggers at the latter's home, he found him enveloped in the same kind of legal atmosphere.

"He cross-examined his very wine when he had nothing else in hand. He held it between himself and the candle, tasted the port, rolled it in his mouth, swallowed it, looked at his glass again, smelt the port, tried it, drank it, filled again, and cross-examined the glass again, until I was as nervous as if I had known the wine to be telling him something to my disadvantage. Three or four times I feebly thought I would start conversation; but whenever he saw me going to ask him anything, he looked at me with his glass in his hand, and rolling his wine about in his mouth, as if requesting me to take notice that it was of no use, for he couldn't answer."

When testimony was needed Jaggers saw to it that witnesses were available. They were prepared to swear, "in a general way, anythink." John Wemmick, his confidential clerk, was an able assistant. As Wemmick said to Pip, in identifying the person whose bust stood in Jaggers' office,

"This chap murdered his master, and considering that he wasn't brought up to evidence, didn't plan it badly."

Nothing succeeds like success and Jaggers was the outstanding criminal lawyer of London during Pip's early manhood. No more finished specimen of legal bully can be found in all literature—perfect in the art of hectoring witnesses, terrifying judges and bamboozling juries.

Wemmick was really quite a remarkable fellow. He had two distinct natures. At the office he was a close-mouthed, stern individual, who gave no evidence of having any sentiment in his make-up. No feeling was allowed to enter into matters entrusted to Jaggers—he was hard as steel and his clerk must be likewise. But when Wemmick left the depressing atmosphere of the office he was an entirely different person.

"Casting my eyes on Mr. Wemmick as we went along, to see what he was like in the light of day, I found him to be a dry man, rather short in stature, with a square wooden face, whose expression seemed to have been imperfectly chipped out with a dull-edged chisel. There were some marks in it which might have been dimples, if the material had been softer and the instrument finer, but which, as it was, were only dents. * * * He wore his hat on the back of his head, and looked straight before him; walking in a self-contained way, as if there were nothing in the streets to claim his attention. His mouth was such a post-office of a mouth that he had a mechanical appearance of smiling."

STRYVER

He lived some miles distant in a little wooden cottage, designed to imitate a fortified castle, and had a collection of curiosities of a "felonious character." His aged father, who had long been stone deaf, lived with him. Wemmick was devoted to the old man and never let up in his efforts to make him comfortable and happy.

Pip was a frequent visitor at Wemmick's house and they grew to be great friends. Wemmick proved to be a valuable advisor of Pip's on all occasions except when the former was discharging the duties of his office as clerk for Jaggers. While so engaged he was austere and non-committal like his master. His devotion to what he called "portable property" was particularly amusing. During his years of service he had acquired a considerable amount of jewelry and other personal property which had been given to him in appreciation of services rendered to clients. Frequently condemned criminals would present Wemmick with some of their personal belongings. As a result of his large accumulation of various kinds of chattels, that kind of property attained great importance in his eyes, and he continually urged Pip to specialize in the acquisition of "portables." Jaggers and Wemmick are outstanding personalities in Dickens' legal world.

Another lawyer of the same general type as Jaggers is Stryver, who makes his appearance in A Tale of Two Cities. A noisy, swaggering sort of person, he assumes importance as the legal representative of Charles Darnay, charged with high treason against the English government. This novel is a romance dealing with political offenses, whereas Great Expectations was grounded in criminal depravity in which most of the central characters were violators of the penal code.

Stryver was a man about thirty years of age, but looked thirty years older. He was:

> "stout, loud, red, bluff, and free from any drawback of delicacy, had a pushing way of shouldering himself (morally and physically) with companies and conversations, that argue well for his shouldering his way up in life."

He was a trial lawyer, as distinguished from the solicitor, whose work was confined to the office. Big and unscrupulous, Stryver lacked the ability to separate the wheat from the chaff—to extract from the mass of evidence the vital facts. This was the service Sydney Carton performed, without which Stryver would have remained in professional obscurity. Carton was a man of both brain and heart, but an idler and a drunkard. He was almost always steeped in liquor, but on hand whenever his employer was engaged in a trial, hands in his pockets, staring at the ceiling. The lion and the jackal, the one in front entirely dependent on the other. This same kind of an alignment is not uncommon today—the aggressive, vociferous trial lawyer, without capacity for careful analysis, whose ammunition is supplied by one more able, but without ambition, and often the victim of his own vices. In creating Jaggers and Stryver, Dickens was evidently modeling them after types prominent in the profession of his day, hulking men, not unwilling to resort to unscrupulous methods to gain their end and able to force their way to the front by reason of their physical strength and dominating personalities.

Stryver is introduced for the first time as counsel for Charles Darnay who was charged with the crime of treason. Darnay, a French nobleman, was a voluntary exile from France, who had renounced his position. The defendant had pleaded not guilty to an indictment denouncing him as a traitor to his country. He was alleged to have furnished the French Government with information relating to England's troops and plans, the two countries being at war at that time. This trial took place in the Old Bailey, the famous criminal court building in London. Witnesses for the prosecution testified to Darnay's frequent trips between England and France. Their evidence left the inference that the prisoner was in fact secretly communicating with representatives of the French Government. It was shown that on one of his trips to France he had traveled back some dozen miles or more to a garrison and dockyard and there collected information. One witness was produced who swore that he had seen Darnay in the coffee room of a certain hotel in that garrison and dockyard town waiting for another person. This testimony was impressive and the jury took particular note of it. However, on cross-examination, Stryver was able to entirely destroy the effect of it, by calling attention to the remarkable resemblance between the prisoner and Sidney Carton. The witness could no longer be sure that it was Darnay he had seen in the coffee room and the defendant was acquitted.

It was not the brain of Stryver that was responsible for this effective cross-examination, but that of the dissolute Carton who sat behind him. Carton, "idlest and most uncompromising of men," was Stryver's greatest ally, prepared the cases, suggested the questions to be propounded to witnesses, and was in fact the strategist upon whom Stryver relied. No recognition came to Carton—Stryver received the plaudits of the crowd and entire credit for the effective manner in which his cases were conducted. Carton, a man of ability, was unable to rise above his own weaknesses and always remained in the background.

After his acquittal Darnay went to France to assist in securing the release of one of his old servants, who had been imprisoned by the revolutionary forces. The French Revolution was in progress at that time. Darnay was himself arrested before he could return to England. He was released through the efforts of Dr. Mannette, his father-in-law, but was promptly rearrested. After a trial before the revolutionary tribunal, he was sentenced to death as an emigrant. Sidney Carton came to France and, through the efforts of one of the jailors with whom he had been acquainted in England, was able to arrange an interview with Darnay in his cell. Carton exchanged places with Darnay and, because of the striking resemblance between them, the latter was able to escape to England. Carton went to the guillotine in his place and thereby became one of the outstanding heroes of all fiction. His unrequited love for Lucy Mannette, the wife of Darney, was the influence that prompted him to make the sacrifice.

Another unsavory legal light created by the pen of Dickens, is Sampson Brass, whose life history is recorded in the pages of Old Curiosity Shop. Here again, is a slippery fellow, large of frame and short of conscience, who offered his services indiscriminately to any rogue seeking to take advantage of his fellow man. What a reflection on the legal profession this man represents and how pleased the reader is to find that virtue is triumphant in the end.

"He was a tall, meager man, with a nose like a wen, a protruding forehead, retreating eyes and hair of a deep red. He wore a long black surtout reaching nearly to his ankles, short black trousers, high shoes and cotton stockings of a bluish grey. He had a cringing manner, but a very harsh voice; and his blandest smiles were so extremely forbidding that to have had his company under the least repulsive circumstances, one would have wished him to be out of temper that he might only scowl.

"It was a maxim with Mr. Brass that the habit of paying compliments kept a man's tongue oiled without any expense; and, as that useful member ought never to grow rusty or creak in turning on its hinges in the case of a practitioner of the law, in whom it should be always glib and easy, he lost few opportunities of improving himself by the utterance of handsome speeches and eulogistic expressions. And this had passed into such a habit with him, that, if he could not be correctly said to have his tongue at his finger's ends, he might certainly be said to have it anywhere but in his face; which being, as we have already seen,

of a harsh and repulsive character, was not oiled so
easily, but frowned above all the smooth speeches—
one of nature's beacons, warning off those who navi-
gated the shoals and breakers of the World, or of
that dangerous strait the Law, and admonishing them
to seek less treacherous harbors and try their fortune
elsewhere."

So the author describes him when he first appears in
the house from which the story gets its name. Little
Nell's grandfather lies there at the point of death and
Quilp, that miserable dwarf, had moved in with Brass
as his legal adviser, to seize the household goods, title
to which had been transferred to Quilp as security for
money loaned to the old man. After his recovery when
he and Little Nell leave the shop in the early morning to
wander abroad, they are obliged to pass through the
storeroom of old curiosities where Brass is sleeping,
and the author very effectively refers to him as "the
ugliest piece of goods in all the store."

Sampson Brass was aided and abetted by his sister,
Miss Sally Brass, "of a gaunt and bony figure and a
resolute bearing," who bore a striking resemblance to
her brother, even to the reddish demonstration carried
on her upper lip.

> "The law had been her nurse. And, as bandy-
> legs or such physical deformities in children are held
> to be the consequence of bad nursing, so, if in a mind
> so beautiful any moral twist or bandiness could be
> found, Miss Sally Brass's nurse was alone to blame."

She had passed her life in a kind of legal childhood,
and although unable to practice on account of her sex,

was a student of the law and an able assistant to her brother.

"In mind, she was of a strong and vigorous turn, having from her earliest youth devoted herself with uncommon ardour to the study of the law; not wasting her speculations upon its eagle flights, which are rare, but tracing it attentively through all the slippery and eel-like crawlings in which it commonly pursues its way."

Dickens' intense dislike for the law and lawyers must have prompted these scathing references to the noble profession.

Quilp, who was Brass's most valuable client, forced the lawyer to hire poor, dilapidated Dick Swiveller as a clerk. In commenting on the desirability of this arrangement, the dwarf said:

"With Miss Sally and the beautiful fictions of the law, his days will pass like minutes. Those charming creations of the poet, John Doe and Richard Roe, when they first dawn upon him, will open a new world for the enlargement of his mind and the improvement of his heart."

Brass maintained his office and home in Bevis Marks in the city of London. He rented a front bedroom to a mysterious stranger, referred to as the Single Gentleman. He later proved to be a brother to Little Nell's grandfather. This man was given to inveigling exhibitors of "Punch" to stage their performances in front of the Brass household and squalid law office. The Single

Gentleman would establish himself in the window of his room, and after the performance always invited the show people into the house for a noisy session, much to the disgust of the solicitor. Brass contrived all sorts of means for dispersing the crowd which collected in front of the building, such as pouring water on their heads, pelting them with fragments of tile and mortar, and bribing cab drivers to dash around the corner and in among them precipitately. He did not resort to law, according to Dickens, because,

> "As Doctors seldom take their own prescriptions, and Divines do not always practice what they preach, so lawyers are shy of meddling with the Law on their own account; knowing it to be an edged tool of uncertain application, very expensive in the working, and rather remarkable for its properties of close shaving than for its always shaving the right person."

A caustic comment on the efficacy of legal procedure as it existed at that day, and still pertinent, notwithstanding the passage of time.

The plot of Old Curiosity Shop is based in the main on the depravity of Daniel Quilp, who utterly hated everybody, good and bad, including Sampson Brass, his own hireling. His efforts to obtain the money which he figured little Nell would inherit at the death of her grandfather, are, of course, finally thwarted. An avaricious and grovelling person, the humor of the characterization of Brass is due to his hypocrisy in posing as a man of virtue. "It isn't the waistcoat that I look at. It is the heart," he says. And again he exclaims with some degree of wisdom, "If there were no bad people, there would be no good lawyers." Convicted of perjury and fraud, sentenced to penal servitude for a period of years, and his name erased from the roll of attorneys, we leave him in the end. And Dickens, unable to forego an opportunity to reflect on the detested profession, says in referring to the disbarment,

"Which erasure has always been held in these latter times to be a great degradation and reproach and to imply the commission of some amazing villainy —as, indeed, would seem to be the case, when so many worthless names remain among its better records, unmolested."

Dick Swiveller, who served Brass as a clerk for a short time, saw everything through the illusions of drink. He was a roistering, shiftless fellow, whose ready flow of words, furnish some of the richest humor to be found in Dickens' works. "What is the odds so long as the fire of soul is kindled at the taper of conwiviality, and the wing of friendship never moults a feather" was his philosophy. Although he plots with Quilp to marry little Nell, in order to get possession of the money which they think she will eventually come into possession of, Swiveller is not at heart a bad fellow. In fact, he finally assists in exposing Brass and the other conspirators, and uses some of the money which was left to him, to educate the Marchioness, illegitimate daughter of Sally Brass and Quilp, who has been abused, maligned and starved all her life. She finally escapes from the Brass household to nurse Swiveller through a siege of brain fever back to health. After

the law office was disrupted by the attorney's imprisonment, Swiveller abandoned his clerical occupation,
inherited an annuity of 150 pounds from his aunt and
married the little Marchioness, to whom he assigned the
name of Sophronia Sphinx, "as being euphonious and
genteel and furthermore indicative of mystery."

Illustrating the ready wit of Swiveller, is his statement to the lodger in the Brass household, who failed
to put in an appearance one morning and was therefore
the subject of a vigorous search on 'the part of
Swiveller and the Brass family.   When they finally
succeeded in arousing him, the lodger becomes indignant
and asks,

> "Is my peace nothing?" "Is their peace nothing,
> Sir?" returned Dick, "I don't wish to hold out any
> threats, sir—indeed, the law does not allow of
> threats, for to threaten is an indictable offense. * * *
> We have been distracted with fear that you were
> dead, Sir, * * * and the short and long of it is,
> that we can not allow single gentlemen to come into
> this establishment and sleep like double gentlemen
> without paying extra for it?" "Indeed!" cried the
> lodger. "Yes, Sir, indeed!" returned Dick, * * *
> "An equal quantity of slumber was never got out of
> one bed and bedstead, and if you're going to sleep in
> that way, you must pay for a double-bedded room."

Given to the purchase of meals and other household
necessities on credit, with subsequent inability to discharge the obligation, Swiveller kept a little book in
which he entered the names of the streets that he was
unable to travel while the shops were open.

"This dinner today closes Longacre. I bought a pair of boots in Great Queen Street last week, and made that no thoroughfare, too. There's only one avenue to the Strand left open now, and I shall have to stop up that tonight with a pair of gloves. The roads are closing so fast in every direction that in about a month's time, unless my aunt sends me a remittance, I shall have to go three or four miles out of town to get over the way."

Although Swiveller was not an articled clerk and little concerned with the law, his nimble brain would have been a distinct asset to any member of the legal profession.

In Old Curiosity Shop we have evidence of Dickens' lack of knowledge of the rules of law as they existed at that time. Daniel Quilp committed suicide and yet Mrs. Quilp, as he left no will, succeeded to his property. As a matter of fact, at the time that Dickens wrote, the property of a felo de se was forfeited to the crown, and even if he had not killed himself, his wife would have inherited only one half his property.

Pettifogging by artists skilled in that line of endeavor is the legal high light in Pickwick Papers. Dodson and Fogg, attorneys of the Courts of King's Bench and solicitors of the High Court of Chancery, play a prominent part, as do those noted trial lawyers, Serjeants Buzfuz and Snubbin. These last two gentlemen are the only members of the higher ranks of the legal profession who are mentioned by Dickens, indicating that he had a limited acquaintance with barristers and King's Counsel. The order of Serjeants at Law was

abolished by the Judicature Act of 1873 which came
into operation in 1875. In the middle ages the Serjeants belonged to an order which took rank as the
highest in the legal profession and from them the King
selected King's Serjeants to represent him in his courts.
King's Counsel gradually replaced the Serjeants. But
one privilege the latter retained down to 1846. They had
the monoply of an audience as pleaders at the Common
Pleas Bar. The Crown attempted to abolish this
monoply in 1834, but the attack was successfully re-
sisted, so that it was necessary for Mrs. Bardell and
Mr. Pickwick to retain Serjeants to represent them.

Dodson and Fogg had presented claim against Mr.
Pickwick for breach of promise of marriage. After receiving a letter from them making a demand for damages, Pickwick decided to call at their offices to find out
upon what facts the claim was grounded. Accompanied
by his faithful and extremely intelligent servant, Sam
Weller, he found upon his arrival at the lawyers' offices
that Dodson was out and Fogg engaged. While waiting in the outer office they overheard a conversation
between the clerks which was quite enlightening,

> " 'There was such a game with Fogg here, this
> mornin', said the man in the brown coat, 'while
> Jack was upstairs sorting the papers, and you two
> were gone to the stamp-office. Fogg was down here,
> opening the letters, when that chap as we issued the
> writ against at Camberwell, you know, came in—
> what's his name again?'
> " 'Ramsey,' said the clerk who had spoken to Mr.
> Pickwick.
> "Ah, Ramsey,—a precious seedy-looking cus-

tomer. 'Well, sir,' says old Fogg, looking at him very fierce—you know his way—'well, sir, have you come to settle?' 'Yes, I have, sir,' said Ramsey, putting his hand in his pocket, and bringing out the money, 'the debt's two pound ten, and the costs three pound five, and here it is, sir;' and he sighed like bricks, as he lugged out the money, done up in a bit of blotting paper. Old Fogg looked first at the money, and then at him, and then he coughed in his rum way, so that I knew something was coming. 'You don't know there's a declaration filed, which increases the costs materially, I suppose?' said Fogg. 'You don't say that, sir' said Ramsey, starting back; 'the time was only out last night, sir.' 'I do say it, though,' said Fogg, 'my clerk's just gone to file it. Hasn't Mr. Jackson gone to file that declaration in Bullman and Ramsey, Mr. Wicks?' Of course I said yes, and then Fogg coughed again, and looked at Ramsey. 'My God!' said Ramsey; 'and here have I nearly driven myself mad, scraping this money together, and all to no purpose.' 'None at all,' said Fogg, coolly: 'so you had better go back and scrape some more together, and bring it here in time.' 'I can't get it, by God,' said Ramsey; striking the desk with his fist. 'Don't bully me, sir,' said Fogg, getting into a passion on purpose. 'I am not bullying you sir,' said Ramsey. 'You are,' said Fogg; 'get out, sir; get out of this office, sir, and come back, sir, when you know how to behave yourself.' Well, Ramsey tried to speak, but Fogg wouldn't let him, so he put the money in his pocket, and sneaked out. The door was scarcely shut, when old Fogg turned round to me, with a sweet smile on his face, and drew the declaration out of his coat pocket. 'Here, Wicks,' says Fogg, 'take a cab, and go down to the Temple as quick as you can, and file that. The costs are quite safe, for he's a steady man with a large family, at a

salary of five-and-twenty shillings a week, and if he
gives us a warrant of attorney, as he must in the end,
I know his employers will see it paid; so we may as
well get all we can out of him, Mr. Wicks; it's a
Christian act to do it, Mr. Wicks, for with his large
family and small income, he'll be all the better for a
good lesson against getting into debt,—won't he Mr.
Wicks won't he?'—and he smiled so good-naturedly
as he went away, that it was delightful to see him.
He is a capital man of business,' said Wicks, in a
tone of deepest admiration, 'capital, isn't he?'

The other three cordially subscribed to this
opinion, and the anecdote afforded the most unlimited
satisfaction.

'Nice men these here, sir,' whispered Mr. Weller
to his master; 'wery nice notion of fun they has, sir.' "

These rascally solicitors persuaded Mrs. Bardell,
with whom Mr. Pickwick boarded for a time, to insti-
tute an action against him for breach of promise. There
was no competent evidence available to support the
claim that Pickwick had ever mentioned marriage to
the woman.

At a conference with his trial lawyer about the case,
Mr. Pickwick indicated that he had a very clear under-
standing of the mechanics of the profession.

" 'Gentlemen of your profession, sir,' continued
Mr. Pickwick, 'see the worst side of human nature—
all its disputes, all its ill-will and bad blood, rise up
before you. You know from your experience of
juries (I mean no disparagement to you, or them)
how much depends upon *effect*; and you are apt to
attribute to others, a desire to use, for purposes of
deception and self-interest, the very instruments

which you, in pure honesty and honor of purpose, and with a laudable desire to do your utmost for your client, know the temper and worth of so well, from constantly employing them yourselves. I really believe that to this circumstance may be attributed the vulgar but very general notion of your being, as a body, suspicious, distrustful, and over-cautious."

These comments are as appropriate today as they were in the 19th century and demonstrate the keenness of Dickens' powers of observation.

The lawyers were able to show that on one occasion Mrs. Bardell had fainted, and called witnesses who saw the defendant holding her in his arms immediately afterwards. A few notes written by Pickwick to the plaintiff were produced and read to the jury. They contained no direct expression of affection, but the lawyers read into them an unwarranted inference that the writer was in fact declaring his love for the woman.

The parties to the action did not go into the box and tell their tale because the law excluded the evidence of all persons interested in the result of the action, and, a fortiori, the parties to the action. This exclusive rule was found in both the civil and canon law, and the common law. In the civil and canon law it was based on the fear that to allow interested persons to testify would be a direct incitement to perjury. This disqualification was eliminated in the nineteenth century. As a result of the rabble rousing appeals of plaintiff's counsel, the jury was induced to return a verdict in her favor in the sum of 750 pounds. The indignant Pickwick refused to pay one cent of the judgment and, as provided by law, was sent to debtor's prison under a body execution.

Some doubt has been expressed as to the propriety of jailing the defendant for his failure to pay the judgment, since he was a man of means. The explanation of this procedure lies in the fact that Pickwick had no lands or tangible chattels. His income was derived from his investments in choses in action that could not be taken under any common law writs then available because they could not be physically seized. The only means of making Pickwick pay was to have him arrested until he settled. It was a master stroke to put further pressure on him by having Mrs. Bardell arrested and sent to the same prison. It was only after Mrs. Bardell had been jailed upon a writ issued by Dodson and Fogg, because of her failure to pay costs due them, that the case was adjusted. She made a written confession that her claim was entirely without merit. As soon as that was done, Pickwick paid the accrued court costs and both of them escaped further servitude.

Undoubtedly the most amusing scene in Dickens' works from the lawyer's standpoint, is the report of the trial of Bardell versus Pickwick. Here is pettifoggery at its best or worst—how often is it duplicated in this country. Serjeant Buzfuz, Mrs. Bardell's counsel, remarkable for his brutal and bullying insolence to the witnesses on Mr. Pickwick's side, is assisted by Mr. Skimpin. Mr. Serjeant Snubbin, assisted by Mr.

Phunky, appear for the defendant. Mr. Justice Starleigh, who presided in the absence of the Chief Justice,
is described as a short man, who seemed all face and
waistcoat. Falling asleep occasionally during the trial,
confounding persons and things and generally exhibit-
ing a considerable amount of mental imbecility, Justice
Starleigh is a caricature, by no means extravagant, of
many judges of our day.

What a distortion of facts was presented by Serjeant
Buzfuz in his opening statement. He began by saying
that never in his whole professional experience had he
approached a case with such a heavy sense of respon-
sibility imposed upon him. He then proceeded to de-
scribe Pickwick as a monster—a serpent on the watch—
and Mrs. Bardell as a lonely and desolate widow. She
had no fear—she had no distrust—she had no suspicion
—all was confidence and reliance. In referring to two
letters written by Pickwick, Serjeant Buzfuz said,

> "And now, gentlemen, but one word more. Two
> letters have passed between these parties, letters
> which are admitted to be in the hand-writing of the
> defendant, and which speak volumes indeed. * * *
> Let me read the first: 'Garraway's, twelve o'clock.
> Dear Mrs. B.—Chops and Tomata sauce. Yours
> Pickwick.' Gentlemen, what does this mean? Chops
> and Tomata sauce. Yours, Pickwick. Chops!
> Gracious heavens! And Tomata sauce! Gentle-
> men, is the happiness of a sensitive and confiding
> female to be trifled away, by such shallow artifices
> as these? The next has no date whatever, which is
> in itself suspicious.—'Dear Mrs. B., I shall not be at
> home until tomorrow. Slow coach.' And then

follows this very, very remarkable expression—
'Don't trouble yourself about the warming-pan.' The
warming-pan! Why, gentlemen, who *does* trouble
himself about a warming-pan? * * * . Why is Mrs.
Bardell so earnestly entreated not to agitate herself
about this warming-pan, unless (as is no doubt the
case) it is a mere cover for hidden fire—a mere sub-
stitute for some endearing word or promise, agree-
ably to a preconcerted system of correspondence,
artfully contrived by Pickwick with a view to his
contemplated desertion, and which I am not in a
condition to explain? * * * .

"But enough of this. * * * . My client's hopes
and prospects are ruined, and it is no figure of speech
to say that her occupation is gone indeed. The bill is
down—but there is no tenant. Eligible single gentlemen pass and re-pass—but there is no invitation for
them to inquire within or without. All is gloom and
silence in the house. * * * . But Pickwick, gentlemen, Pickwick, the ruthless destroyer of this domestic
oasis in the desert of Goswell Street,—Pickwick, who
has choked up the well, and thrown ashes on the
sward—Pickwick who comes before you today with
his heartless Tomato sauce and warming pans—
Pickwick still rears his head with unblushing
effrontery, and gazes without a sigh on the ruin he
has made. Damages, gentlemen—heavy damages is
the only punishment with which you can visit him; the
only recompense you can award to my client. And for
those damages she now appeals to an enlightened, a
high-minded, a right-feeling, a conscientious, a dis-
passionate, a sympathizing, a contemplative jury of
her civilized countrymen."

That this impassioned appeal in the form of an opening statement was effective, is evidenced by the substan-

tial amount of damages which the jury awarded plain-tiff.

The dangers of indulging in too extended a cross-examination are also aptly illustrated in the report of this trial. After calling several of the defendant's associates to the stand to prove that Mr. Pickwick had been seen holding Mrs. Bardell in his arms on one occasion, Serjeant Buzfuz called Samuel Weller as a witness. He had been boots at the White Hart Inn before becoming valet to Mr. Pickwick. This man made up in mental acuteness what he lacked in grammatical ability, a fact unknown to the plaintiff's attorney. Failing to elicit any helpful information from the witness in his preliminary questions, Serjeant Buzfuz finally obtained from Weller a statement that he had called on Mrs. Bardell a short time before the case came on for trial.

" 'Well; I suppose you went up to have a little talk about this trial—eh, Mr. Weller?' said Serjeant Buzfuz, looking knowingly at the jury.

" 'I went up to pay the rent; but we *did* get a talkin' about the trial,' replied Sam.

" 'Oh, you did get a talking about the trial,' said Serjeant Buzfuz, brightening up with the anticipation of some important discovery. 'Now what passed about the trial; will you have the goodness to tell us, Mr. Weller?'

" 'Vith all the pleasure in life, sir' replied Sam. 'Arter a few unimportant obserwations from the two wirtuous females as has been examined here today, the ladies gets into a wery great state o' admiration at the honorable conduct of Mr. Dodson and Fogg—them two gen'lm'n as is settin' near you now.'

"This, of course, drew general attention to Dodson and Fogg, who looked as virtuous as possible.

" 'The attorneys for the plaintiff,' said Serjeant Buzfuz; 'well, they spoke in high praise of the honourable conduct of Messrs. Dodson and Fogg, the attorneys for the plaintiff, did they?'

" 'Yes,' said Sam, 'they said what a wery gen'rous thing it was o' them to have taken up the case on spec, and to charge nothin' at all for costs, unless they got 'em out of Mr. Pickwick.'

"At this very unexpected reply, the spectators tittered again, and Dodson and Fogg, turning very red, leant over to Serjeant Buzfuz, and in a hurried manner whispered something in his ear.

" 'You are quite right,' said Serjeant Buzfuz aloud, with affected composure. 'It's perfectly useless, my Lord, attempting to get at any evidence through the impenetrable stupidity of this witness. I will not trouble the court by asking him any more questions. Stand down, sir.'

" 'Would any other gen'lm'n like to ask me any-thin'?' inquired Sam, taking up his hat, and looking round most deliberately.

" 'Not I, Mr. Weller, thank you,' said Serjeant Snubbin, laughing."

Weller's keen sense of humor is further illustrated by the following bit of testimony:

" 'Do you recollect anything particular happening on the morning when you were first engaged by the defendant, eh, Mr. Weller?' said Serjeant Buzfuz.

" 'Yes, I do, sir,' replied Sam.

" 'Have the goodness to tell the jury what it was.'

" 'I had a reg'lar new fit out o' clothes that morn-in', gen'lmen of the jury,' said Sam, 'and that was a wery partickler and uncommon circumstance vith me in those days.'

"Hereupon there was a general laugh; and the little judge, looking with an angry countenance over his desk, said, 'You had better be careful, sir.'

" 'So Mr .Pickwick said at the time, my Lord,' replied Sam, 'And I was wery careful o' that 'ere suit o' clothes; wery careful indeed, my Lord.'

'The judge looked sternly at Sam for full two minutes, but Sam's features were so perfectly calm and serene that the judge said nothing, and motioned Serjeant Buzfuz to proceed."

Representing Mr. Pickwick in the capacity of solicitor, is little Mr. Perker, an educated and intelligent gentleman, who made every effort to keep his clients from becoming involved in the expense and uncertainty of litigation. "He carried his black kid gloves *in* his hands not *on* them; and as he spoke thrust his wrists beneath his coat tails with the air of a man who was in the habit of propounding some regular posers." Mr. Perker typifies the highly ethical lawyer who performs a real service to the community. Unfortunately his activities and philosophy are overshadowed by the blustering pettifoggers appearing for the complainant.

In Pickwick Papers we also meet Solomon Pell, an attorney in the Insolvent Court, who assisted Sam Weller to get into the debtor's prison in order to continue his services to Mr. Pickwick. In 1813 Parliament passed an act creating a court for the relief of insolvent debtors which sat in Portugal Street, Lincoln's Inn Fields. We get a picture of the practitioners before it and the actual appearance of the court in this work.

"In a lofty room, badly lighted and worse venti-
lated, situate in Portugal Street, Lincoln's Inn-fields,
there sit, nearly the whole year round, one, two, three,
or four gentlemen in wigs, as the case may be, with
little writing-desks before them, constructed after
the fashion of those used by the judges of the land,
barring the French polish. There is a box of barristers on their right hand; there is an inclosure of
insolvent debtors on their left; and there is an in-
clined plane of most especially dirty faces in their
front. These gentlemen are the Commissioners of
the Insolvent Court, and the place in which they sit
is the Insolvent Court itself.

"It is, and has been, time out of mind, the remarkable fate of this Court to be, somehow or other, held
and understood, by the general consent of all the
destitute shabby-genteel people in London, as their
common resort, and place of daily refuge. It is
always full. The steams of beer and spirits per-
petually ascend to the ceiling, and, being condensed
by the heat, roll down the walls like rain; there are
more old suits of clothes in it at one time than will be
offered for sale in all Houndsditch in a twelvemonth;
more unwashed skins and grizzly beards than all the
pumps and shaving-shops between Tyburn and White-
chapel could render decent, between sunrise and
sunset.

*   *   *

"But the attorneys, who sit at a large, bare table
below the Commissioners, are, after all, the greatest
curiosities. The professional establishment of the
more opulent of these gentlemen consists of a blue
bag and a boy, generally a youth of the Jewish per-
suasion. They have no fixed offices, their legal business being transacted in the parlours of public-houses,
or the yards of prisons, whither they repair in crowds,

and canvass for customers after the manner of omnibus cads. They are of a greasy and mildewed appearance; and if they can be said to have any vices at all, perhaps drinking and cheating are the most conspicuous among them. Their residences are usually on the outskirts of 'the Rules,' chiefly lying within a circle of one mile from the obelisk of St. George's Fields. Their looks are not prepossessing, and their manners are peculiar."

Pell was subsequently retained to give legal effect to the testamentary disposition of Mrs. Weller, the elder. Here again we have evidence that Dickens was not a lawyer, inasmuch as under the law as it existed at that time, Mrs. Weller probably had no right to make a will unless she had a settlement, for the reason that on marriage her property would have passed to her husband. Dickens gives us a very graphic picture of lawyer Pell:

"Mr. Solomon Pell, one of this learned body, was a fat, flabby, pale man, in a surtout, which looked green one minute and brown the next, with a velvet collar of the same chameleon tints. His forehead was narrow, his face wide, his head large, and his nose all on one side, as if Nature, indignant with the propensities she observed in him in his birth, had given it an angry tweak which it had never recovered. Being short-necked and asthmatic, however, he respired principally through this feature; so perhaps, what it wanted in ornament, it made up in usefulness."

Upon the death of Sam Weller's mother-in-law, Pell is hired to probate the will. In order to make the necessary arrangements with the attorney, the elder Weller and his son go to a public house, from which point they dispatched a messenger to the Insolvent Court, request-

ing Pell to call on them immediately. The messenger
found the lawyer munching on a saveloy or dried
sausage in complete idleness. When he was advised
that his services were wanted, he hurried over the way
with such alacrity that he reached the parlor, where his
clients were awaiting him, before the messenger had
even left the court room.

" 'Gentlemen,' said Mr. Pell, touching his hat,
'My service to you all. I don't say it to flatter you,
gentlemen, but there are not five other men in the
world that I'd have come out of that court for today.'

" 'So busy eh?' said Sam.

" 'Busy' replied Pell, 'I'm completely sewn up, as
my friend the late Lord Chancellor many a time used
to say to me, gentlemen, when he came out from hear-
ing appeals in the House of Lords. Poor fellow! he
was very susceptible of fatigue; he used to feel those
appeals uncommonly. I actually thought more than
once that he'd have sunk under 'em; I did indeed.'

"Here Mr. Pell shook his head and paused; on
which, the elder Mr. Weller, nudging his neighbor, as
begging him to mark the attorney's high connexions,
asked whether the duties in question produced any
permanent ill effects on the constitution of his noble
friend.

" 'I don't think he ever quite recovered them,'
replied Pell, 'In fact, I'm sure he never did.' 'Pell,'
he used to say to me many a time, 'How the blazes
you can stand the head work you do, is a mystery to
me.'—'Well,' I used to answer, 'I hardly know how
I do it upon my life.'—'Pell,' he'd add, sighing and
looking at me with a little envy,—friendly envy, you
know, gentlemen, mere friendly envy; I never minded
it,—'Pell, you're a wonder; a wonder.' 'Ah.' you'd
have liked him very much if you had known him,

gentlemen.   Bring me three penn'orth of rum, my dear.' "

How true to life this pen and ink sketch is and how common are the qualities of mind disclosed by Mr. Pell. The same methods to impress the uninitiated are uniformly employed today. We leave this lawyer well fortified with porter, cold beef and oysters and in possession of a fee on which he boarded, lodged and washed for six months afterwards. Even in the recurring descriptions of feasting and drinking, about which much is said in many of his novels—and how effectively does he arouse the appetite—Dickens does not lower the high plane of his literary style. As someone has well said, "He was able to make the stomach an organ of the soul." While too much food and drink produce obesity, his philosophy is found in the words of the elder Weller, whose "face however had expanded, under the influence of good living, and a disposition remarkable for resignation; and its bold fleshy curves had so far extended beyond the limits originally assigned to them, that unless you took a full view of his countenance in front, it was difficult to distinguish more than the extreme tip of a very rubicund nose." He sagely remarked: "Vidth and visdom, Sammy, alvays grows together." It was Sam's father, who in advising Sam about legacies, said:

> "It's a rum sort o' thing, Sammy, to go hangerin' arter anybody's property, ven you're assistin' 'em in illness. It's like helpin' an outside passenger up, ven he's been pitched off a coach, and puttin' your hand in his pocket, vile you ask him vith a sigh how he finds his-self, Sammy."

One of the few firms of lawyers to whom no misconduct is attributed is that of Spenlow and Jorkins, introduced in Dickens' masterpiece, David Copperfield. Spenlow, to whom David was articled, was the father of his beloved Dora—his child wife. Jorkins was a mild man of heavy temperament, whose chief function was to remain in the background and be exhibited to the world by his partner as a harsh and obstinate fellow. Spenlow was always willing to raise the wages of an employee, to reduce a client's fee bill and do other acts of generosity, but he was prevented from doing so by the grasping Jorkins. Thus it was that Jorkins was the unwitting cause of many heartaches.

The firm were Proctors in Doctors' Commons—practitioners in the Admiralty, Ecclesiastical and Probate Courts, where Dickens was employed as a reporter.

> "We were a little like undertakers, in the Commons, as regarded Probate transactions; generally making it a rule to look more or less cut up, when we had to deal with clients in mourning. In a similar feeling of delicacy, we were always blithe and lighthearted with the licence clients."

David was bound by articles of agreement to these lawyers for instruction in law and remained with them a number of years. He finally left their employment and became a writer, just as Dickens abandoned his clerkship to take up newspaper work. In fact David and the author are said to be one and the same person. Spenlow, with whom David had rather close contact because he was courting the lawyer's daughter, frequently stated that all of his affairs were in perfect order and his family well provided for. He sought to impress upon David the desirability of making a will and having one's business so arranged as to be prepared for the inevitable. When he died very suddenly, it was discovered that he had not made any will and had also been living beyond his means. His daughter was left without any resources whatsoever and was obliged to live with her maiden aunts until she married David.

We are also introduced in this book to another lawyer, whose professional life was blameless, although his character was somewhat weak. Mr. Wickfield was a country practitioner—a solicitor in Canterbury. He was a friend and confidential adviser to David's great-aunt, Betsy Trotwood, and on account of that relationship was entrusted with considerable money belonging to her. Wickfield was grief-stricken on account of the death of his wife and subsequently drank so heavily with a resulting neglect of his affairs, that his clerk, Uriah Heep, was able to worm his way into his business secrets, compel Wickfield to make him a partner, and finally to almost completely ruin him by embezzling trust funds. Wickfield was the father of Agnes, that gentle soul who became David Copperfield's second wife. Loyal and faithful to her father, she was always a trusted adviser of Copperfield's.

Uriah Heep, whose name is synonymous with false humility, is as detestable a rogue as you will find within the pages of any novel. As a clerk for Mr. Wickfield, he contrived to become his partner by a series of dishonest maneuvers, craftily robbing him and his clients until exposed by the gallant Micawber.   Heep was a cadaverous fellow, without eyebrows and eyelashes, and had long skeleton hands.   He lived with his mother and continually called attention to his humbleness.

> " 'I am well aware that I am the umblest person going,' said Uriah Heep modestly, 'let the other be where he may.   My mother is likewise a very umble person.   We live in an umble abode, Master Copper-field, but have much to be thankful for.   My father's former calling was umble.   He was a sexton.' "

J. Wilkins Micawber, a sanguine but easily depressed gentleman, originally engaged in the business of a corn chandler and afterwards a clerk for Wickfield and Heep, was responsible for Heep's downfall. Micawber was a total failure as a business man, was always heavily involved in debt, and finally was imprisoned on a body execution.   Given to eloquent speeches and frequent letter writing in a similar vein, his efforts to devise plans which would enable him to earn a living are highly amusing.   Despite the fact that he had been unable to sustain his family in any degree of comfort, Mrs. Micawber clung to him and continually exclaimed that she would never desert him.   Copperfield lived with the Micawber family when he first moved to London and a strong bond of friendship grew up between them.   Micawber was a man of variable spirits, fond of conviviality and always waiting for something to turn up.

> "I went in and found there a stoutish, middle-aged person, in a brown surtout and black tights and shoes;

with no more hair upon his head (which was a large one and very shining) than there is upon an egg, and with a very extensive face, which he turned full upon me. His clothes were shabby, but he had an imposing shirt collar on. He carried a jaunty sort of a stick, with a large pair of rusty tassels to it; and a quizzing glass hung outside his coat,—for ornament I afterwards found, as he very seldom looked through it, and couldn't see anything when he did."

After trying many occupations, Micawber finally became a clerk for Uriah Heep and the crowning achievement of his otherwise drab career, is his exposure of Heep's dishonesty. He carefully collected all of the necessary incriminating evidence and then called upon David to advise him of the situation. When the latter saw Micawber approaching, he knew instantly that something was wrong. In response to his inquiry as to what was the matter, Micawber replied with great feeling:

"Villainy is the matter; baseness is the matter; deception, fraud, conspiracy are the matter; and the name of the whole atrocious mass is—Heep."

Micawber and Copperfield, accompanied by Traddles, thereupon repaired to the office of Wickfield and Heep, where all of the dishonesty of the junior partner was exposed by Micawber. As a result Mr. Wickfield recovered all of the property of which he had been defrauded and afterwards Heep was sentenced to prison for a term of years. Shortly after this exposure Micawber gave up his clerical work and emigrated with his entire family to Australia, where he finally became a magistrate and lived happily to a ripe old age.

Thomas Traddles, who was one of David's school-mates at Salem House, also plays a rather prominent part in this romance. He had a rather difficult child-hood and in his school days was always being caned by Mr. Creakle, an ignorant and cruel master in charge of the boarding school, who believed in solitary confine-ment and strict discipline. Traddles was continually threatening to write home to his uncle about the abuses which were heaped upon him, but never did so.

"In a tight sky-blue suit that made his arms and legs like German sausages or roly poly puddings, he was the merriest and most miserable of all the boys."

Traddles finally succeeded in gaining admission to the bar and eventually became a judge of high honor and esteem.

In Bleak House, Dickens sought to expose the evil effects of delayed justice. The case of Jarndyce versus Jarndyce had been in the court of chancery for genera-tions. It had been the despair and ruin of so much hope and so many lives and only came to an end when the whole estate had been eaten up in costs. One of the Jarndyce family made a large fortune and had drawn for him an involved will, creating a number of trusts. John Jarndyce aptly described the famous case to his ward:

"It's about a Will, and the trusts under a Will—or it was, once. It's about nothing but Costs, now. We are always appearing, and disappearing, and swear-ing, and interrogating, and filing, and cross-filing,

and arguing, and sealing, and motioning, and referring, and reporting, and revolving about the Lord
Chancellor and all his satellites, and equitably waltz-
ing ourselves off to dusty death, about Costs. That's
the great question. All the rest, by some extra-
ordinary means, has melted away. * * *

"A certain Jarndyce, in an evil hour, made a great
fortune, and made a great Will. In the question how
the trusts under that Will are to be administered, the
fortune left by the Will is squandered away; the lega-
tees under the Will are reduced to such a miserable
condition that they would be sufficiently punished if
they had committed an enormous crime in having
money left them; and the Will itself is made a dead
letter. All through the deplorable cause, everything
that everybody in it, except one man, knows already,
is referred to that only one man who don't know it, to
find out—all through the deplorable cause, everybody must have copies, over and over again, of everything that has accumulated about it in the way of
cartloads of papers (or must pay for them without
having them, which is the usual course, for nobody
wants them) ; and must go down the middle and up
again, through such an infernal country-dance of
costs and fees and nonsense and corruption as was
never dreamed of in the wildest visions of a Witch's
Sabbath. * * * . And we can't get out of the suit
on any terms, for we are made parties to it and *must
be* parties to it, whether we like or not. But it won't
do to think of it ! When my great-uncle, poor Tom
Jarndyce, began to think of it, it was the beginning
of the end !' "

In the first chapter of the book Dickens gives us a
graphic picture of a session of the Lord High Chancellor in his High Court of Chancery:

"The raw afternoon is rawest, and the dense fog
is densest, and the muddy streets are muddiest, near
that leaden-headed old obstruction, appropriate ornament for the threshold of a leaden-headed old cor-
poration—Temple Bar. And hard by Temple Bar,
in Lincoln's Inn Hall, at the very heart of the fog,
sits the Lord High Chancellor in his High Court of
Chancery.

"Never can there come fog too thick, never can
there come mud and mire too deep, to assort with
the groping and floundering condition which this
High Court of Chancery, most pestilent of hoary
sinners, holds, this day, in the sight of heaven and
earth.

"On such an afternoon, if ever, the Lord High
Chancellor ought to be sitting here—as here he is—
with a foggy glory round his head, softly fenced in
with crimson cloth and curtains, addressed by a large
advocate with great whiskers, a little voice, and an
interminable brief, and outwardly directing his con-
templation to the lantern in the roof, where he can
see nothing but fog. On such an afternoon, some
score of members of the High Court of Chancery Bar
ought to be—as here they are—mistily engaged in
one of the ten thousand stages of an endless cause,
tripping one another up on slippery precedents, groping knee-deep in technicalities, running their goat-
hair and horse-hair warded heads against walls of
words, and making a pretence of equity with serious
faces, as players might. On such an afternoon, the
various solicitors in the cause, some two or three of
whom have inherited it from their fathers, who made
a fortune by it, ought to be—as are they not?—
ranged in a line, in a long matted well (but you might
look in vain for Truth at the bottom of it), between
the registrar's red table and the silk gowns, with bills,
cross-bills, answers, rejoinders, injunctions, affidavits,

issues, references to masters, masters' reports, mountains of costly nonsense, piled before them. Well may the court be dim, with wasting candles here and there; well may the fog hang heavy in it, as if it would never get out; well may the stained glass windows lose their colour, and admit no light of day into the place; well may the uninitiated from the streets, who peep in through the glass panes in the door, be deterred from entrance by its owlish aspect, and by the drawl languidly echoing to the roof from the padded dais where the Lord High Chancellor looks into the lantern that has no light in it, and where the attendant wigs are all stuck in a fog-bank! This is the Court of Chancery; which has its decaying houses and its blighted lands in every shire; which has its worn-out lunatic in every madhouse, and its dead in every churchyard; which has its ruined suitor, with his slipshod heels and threadbare dress, borrowing and begging through the round of every man's acquaintance; which gives to moneyed might the means abundantly of wearying out the right; which so exhausts finances, patience, courage, hope, so overthrows the brain and breaks the heart, that there is not an honourable man among its practitioners who would not give—who does not often give—the warning, 'Suffer any wrong that can be done you, rather than come here.' "

Dickens was obsessed with the idea that the one great object of English law was to make business for itself.

"Let them but once clearly perceive that its grand principle is to make business for itself at their expense, and surely they will cease to grumble."

In his zeal to condemn the bad effects of justice deferred, he lost sight of the fact that the establishment of courts of equity represented a great step forward in the jurisprudence of his country. As Keeper of the King's Conscience, the Chancellor was expected to give relief where none was available before, because of the intricacies of procedure in the courts of common law. It must be confessed, however, that the author's description of the workings of the Court of Chancery is an impressive one, and the book was an important factor in bringing about procedural reforms in the English courts. It took about one hundred years to accomplish the change. The agitation really commenced in 1776 and continued down through the nineteenth century until the passage of the Judicature Acts, regarded as models of effective procedure. Dickens' novel, dramatizing the delays of Chancery, unquestionably hastened the enactment of the corrective legislation. He sensed the great wrong that always resulted from protracted litigation, and, while his description of the Court of Chancery was perhaps exaggerated in some respects, his exposure of the law's delay was both accurate and impressive.

His ability to portray people, institutions and events placed him near the crest of Parnassus. He displayed unusual power in Bleak House, not only in constructing the plot and weaving the characters, but also in describing the courts, both in term time and out. Satire, of which he was a master, is employed and this is all the more reason for paying tribute to his great intellect. It must be handled by an artist to be effective. In the hands of anyone else it is deplorable. Dickens' sketch of Chancery Lane, after the adjournment of the courts for the summer, is a flawless bit of literature.

"It is the long vacation in the regions of Chancery Lane. The good ships Law and Equity, those teak-built, copper-bottomed, iron-fastened, brazen-faced, and not by any means fast-sailing clippers, are laid up in ordinary. The Flying Dutchman, with a crew of ghostly clients imploring all whom they may encounter to peruse their papers, has drifted, for the time being, Heaven knows where. The courts are all shut up; the public offices lie in a hot sleep; Westminister Hall itself is a shady solitude where nightingales might sing, and a tenderer class of suitors than is usually found there, walk.

"The Temple, Chancery Lane, Serjeants' Inn, and Lincoln's Inn, even unto the Fields, are like tidal harbours at low water; where stranded proceedings, offices at anchor, idle clerks lounging on lop-sided stools that will not recover their perpendicular until the current of Term sets in, lie high and dry upon the ooze of the long vacation. Outer doors of chambers are shut up by the score, messages and parcels are to be left at the Porter's Lodge by the bushel. A crop of grass would grow in the chinks of the stone pavement outside Lincoln's Inn Hall, but that the ticket-porters, who have nothing to do beyond sitting in the shade there, with their white aprons over their heads to keep the flies off, grub it up and eat it thoughtfully.

"There is only one Judge in town. Even he only comes twice a week to sit in chambers. If the country folks of those assize towns on his circuit could see him now! No full-bottomed wig, no red petticoats, no fur, no javelin-men, no white wands. Merely a close-shaved gentleman in white trousers and a white hat, with sea-bronze on the judicial countenance, and a strip of bark peeled by the solar rays from the judicial nose, who calls in at the shell-fish shop as he comes along, and drinks iced ginger beer!

"The bar of England is scattered over the face of the earth. How England can get on through four long summer months without its bar—which is its acknowledged refuge in adversity and its only legitimate triumph in prosperity—is beside the question; assuredly that shield and buckler of Britannia are not in present wear. The learned gentleman who is always so tremendously indignant at the unprecedented outrage committed on the feelings of his client by the opposite party, that he never seems likely to recover it, is doing infinitely better than might be expected, in Switzerland. The learned gentleman who does the withering business, and who blights all opponents with his gloomy sarcasm, is as merry as a grig at a French watering-place. The learned gentleman who weeps by the pint on the smallest provocation has not shed a tear these six weeks. The very learned gentleman who has cooled the natural heat of his gingery complexion in pools and fountains of law, until he has become great in knotty arguments for Term-time, when he poses the drowsy Bench with legal 'chaff,' inexplicable to the uninitiated and to most of the initiated, too, is roaming, with a characteristic delight in aridity and dust, about Constantinople. Other dispersed fragments of the same great Palladium are to be found on the canals of Venice, at the second cataract of the Nile, in the baths of Germany, and sprinkled on the seasand all over the English coast. Scarcely one is to be encountered in the deserted region of Chancery Lane. If such a lonely member of the bar do flit across the waste, and come upon a prowling suitor who is unable to leave off haunting the scenes of his anxiety, they frighten one another, and retreat into opposite shades.

"It is the hottest long vacation known for many years. All the young clerks are madly in love, and, according to their various degrees, pine for bliss with the beloved object, at Margate, Ramsgate, or Gravesend. All the middle-aged clerks think their families too large. All the unowned dogs who stray into the Inns of Court, and pant about staircases and other dry places, seeking water, give short howls of aggravation. All the blind men's dogs in the streets draw their masters against pumps, or trip them over buckets. A shop with a sun-blind, and a watered pavement, and a bowl of gold and silver fish in the window, is a sanctuary. Temple Bar gets so hot that it is, to the adjacent Strand and Fleet Street, what a heater is in an urn, and keeps them simmering all night."

The author, with his remarkable talent for looking into the hearts of men, was keenly aware of the great struggle ahead of those who aspired to fame and fortune in the legal world. In describing the Lawyers' Inns, where the prospective barrister was housed, he wrote:

"What do *you* know of the time when young men shut themselves up in those lonely rooms and read and read, hour after hour, and night after night, till their reason wandered beneath their midnight studies; till their mental powers were exhausted; till morning's light brought no freshness or health to them; and they sank beneath the unnatural devotion of their youthful energies to their dry old books? Coming down to a later time, and a very different day, what do *you* know of the gradual sinking beneath consump-

tion or the quick wasting of fever—the grand results
of 'life' and dissipation—which men have undergone
in these same rooms? How many vain pleaders for
mercy, do you think have turned away heart-sick from
the lawyer's office to find a resting-place in the Thames
or a refuge in the gaol? They are no ordinary
houses, those. There is not a panel in the old wain-
scoting, but what, if it were endowed with the powers
of speech and memory, could start from the wall, and
tell its tale of horror—the romance of life, sir, the
romance of life! Common-place as they may seem
now, I tell you they are strange old places, and I
would rather hear many a legend with a terrific
sounding name, than the true history of one old set
of chambers. * * *

"Look at them in another light: their most common-place and least romantic. What fine places of
slow torture they are! Think of the needy man who
has spent his all, beggared himself, and pinched his
friends, to enter the profession, which will never yield
him a morsel of bread. The waiting—the hope—the
disappointment—the fear—the misery—the poverty
—the blight on his hopes, and end to his career—the
suicide perhaps, or the shabby, slipshod drunkard.
Am I not right about them?"

Here is a tragic but accurate picture of the unsuccess-
ful lawyer—the flight of time has in no way changed it.
And equally doleful is his description of the seasoned
practitioner:

"Like a dingy London bird among the birds at
roost in these pleasant fields, where the sheep are all
made into parchment, the goats into wigs, and the
pasture into chaff, the lawyer, smoke-dried and faded,
dwelling among mankind but not consorting with
them, aged without experience of genial youth, and

so long used to make his cramped nest in holes and corners of human nature that he has forgotten its broader and better range, comes sauntering home. In the oven made by the hot pavements and hot buildings, he has baked himself dryer than usual; and he has, in his thirsty mind, his mellowed port-wine, half a century old."

The chancery lawyer, Mr. Vholes, legal representative of Richard Carstone, whose character is ruined by the interminable legal proceedings incident to Jarndyce versus Jarndyce, and the firm of Kenge and Carboy of Lincoln's Inn, make their appearance in this book, always in connection with some legal phase of the same case. These lawyers, according to the author, were respected despite their connection with an infamous proceeding. In telling why Mr. Vholes was respected, Dickens says:

"He is allowed by the greater attorneys who have made good fortunes, or are making them, to be a most respectable man. He never misses a chance in his practice; which is a mark of respectability. He never takes any pleasure; which is another mark of respectability. He is reserved and serious; which is another mark of respectability. His digestion is impaired; which is highly respectable. And he is making hay of the grass which is flesh, for his three daughters. And his father is dependent on him in the Vale of Taunton."

Judged by these standards, the legal profession of our day counts among its members many men of absolute respectability.

Mr. Kenge, of the firm of Kenge and Carboy, was known as conversation Kenge, due to the fact that he lost no chance to talk. He was the senior member of the firm, a portly and important looking gentleman, dressed all in black, with a white cravat, large gold watch seals, pair of gold eyeglasses, and a large seal ring upon his little finger.

"He appeared to enjoy beyond everything the sound of his own voice. * * * I couldn't wonder at that, for it was mellow and full, and gave great importance to every word he uttered. He listened to himself with obvious satisfaction, and sometimes gently beat time to his own music with his head, or rounded a sentence with his hand."

Those who frequently come in contact with the bench and bar will appreciate the accuracy of this portrayal.

The most impressive lawyer to be introduced in Bleak House is Tulkinghorn, legal advisor of the Dedlocks, aristocrats of their day.

"Here, beneath the painted ceiling, with foreshortened Allegory staring down at his intrusion as if it meant to swoop upon him, and he cutting it dead, Mr. Tulkinghorn has at once his house and office. He keeps no staff; only one middle-aged man, usually a little out at the elbows, who sits in a high Pew in the hall, and is rarely overburdened with business. Mr. Tulkinghorn is not in a common way. He wants no clerks. He is a great reservoir of confidences, not to be so tapped. His clients want *him*; he is all in all. Drafts that he requires to be drawn, are drawn by special pleaders in the Temple on

mysterious instructions; fair copies that he requires
to be made, are made at the stationer's, expense being
no consideration. The middle-aged man in the Pew
knows scarcely more of the affairs of the Peerage,
than any crossing-sweeper in Holborn."

He was a high-minded barrister of the old school,
who had become very rich in arranging marriage settle-
ments among the wealthy and in probating their estates.
He was rusty to look at and wore knee breeches tied
with ribbons and gaiters or stockings.

"One peculiarity of his black clothes, and of his
black stockings, be they silk or worsted, is, that they
never shine. Mute, close, irresponsive to any glanc-
ing light, his dress is like himself. He never con-
verses, when not professionally consulted. He is
found sometimes, speechless but quite at home, at
corners of dinner-tables in great country houses, and
near doors of drawing-rooms, concerning which the
fashionable intelligence is eloquent; where everybody
knows him, and where half the Peerage stops to say
'How do you do, Mr. Tulkinghorn?' he receives
these salutations with gravity, and buries them along
with the rest of his knowledge."

Tulkinghorn was familiar with all of the scandal of
his day. After a prolonged investigation he learned the
secret of Lady Dedlock, wife of a wealthy nobleman,
much older than herself. She was the mother of Esther
Summerson by Captain Hawdon, a gay rake, who abandoned the woman without marriage. On informing
Lady Dedlock of his discovery and of his intention to
reveal it to Sir Leicester Dedlock, she fled from her
home and was found dead in the graveyard where

Hawdon lay buried. Shortly afterwards, Tulkinghorn was murdered in his room by a French waiting maid employed by the Dedlocks. He had made use of her to discover certain family secrets and refused to reward her in the amount she desired. The ferreting out of Lady Dedlock's secret is the central theme of this book, involving all of the characters.

Connected with the firm of Kenge and Carboy, as a lawyer's clerk, is William Guppy, usually spoken of as "the young man of the name of Guppy." He conceives a passion for Esther Summerson, the heroine of the story, and suddenly declares his love for her on one occasion when she calls at the office where he his employed. She refuses to accept him and, though greatly disappointed, he does not quite despair. On taking leave he tells her:

> "In case you should think better—at any time, however distant, *that's* no consequence, for my feelings can never alter—of anything I have said, particularly what might I not do—Mr. William Guppy, eighty-seven Penton Place, or, if removed or dead (of blighted hopes or anything of that sort), care of Mrs. Guppy, three hundred and two, Old Street Road, will be sufficient."

Sometime later Miss Summerson calls on Guppy and he notices that she has lost most of her former beauty, due to a serious illness. He thinks that she has called to accept his original proposal of marriage and becomes very much disturbed. Although the young woman assures him that such is not the case, he nevertheless insists that she make a very complete statement before a witness that there never has been any engagement or promise to marry between them.

In Dickens' gallery of lawyers' clerks, Guppy is the most finished picture. He is the perfect type of cockney —with ambition. His speech is modeled on the epistolary style of lawyers' letters or on their spoken style in court, for his sole education was in a lawyer's office. He must have been industrious and able for Kenge and Carboy gave him his articles. He supported his vulgar and not very pleasant old mother and befriended Tony Jobling when he was down on his luck. Subsequent to his service as a clerk, Guppy became a practitioner at the bar. He is an important figure in the plot to uncover Lady Dedlock's early history.

Lowten, Perker's clerk, "a puffy-faced young man," discovered by Pickwick presiding at a sing-song at the Magpie and Stump, at which sundry other lawyers' clerks were present, is the type of efficient managing clerk. So too is Jackson, Dodson and Fogg's outdoor clerk, who served subpoenas on Pickwick's friends and later assisted at the arrest of Mrs. Bardell. Bart Smallweed, lawyer's clerk and friend of Guppy and Anthony Jobling, attracted considerable attention. In describing Smallweed, Dickens says:

> "In short, in his bringing up, he has been so nursed by Law and Equity that he has become a kind of fossil Imp, to account for whose terrestrial existence it is reported at the public offices that his father was John Doe, and his mother the only female member of the Roe family; also that his first long-clothes were made from a blue bag."

The judiciary also came in for unfavorable comment. His description of Justice Starleigh, the pompous and befuddled judge, who presided at the trial of Bardell versus Pickwick, has already been set forth.

In Oliver Twist, we are introduced to a discourteous magistrate before whom Oliver is brought on the charge of picking a handkerchief from Mr. Brownlow's pocket. Oliver was the innocent victim of the criminal band led by Fagin and Mr. Brownlow was a courteous, old gentleman who befriended Oliver, recognizing that he was without blame. Dickens gives us the following description of this jurist:

"Mr. Fang was a lean, long-backed, stiff-necked, middle-sized man, with no great quantity of hair, and what he had, growing on the back and sides of his head. His face was stern, and much flushed. If he were really not in the habit of drinking rather more than was exactly good for him, he might have brought an action against his countenance for libel, and have recovered heavy damages.

"The old gentleman bowed respectfully; and advancing to the magistrate's desk, said, suiting the action to the word,

" 'That is my name and address, sir.' He then withdrew a pace or two; and, with another polite and gentlemanly inclination of the head, awaited to be questioned.

"Now, it so happened that Mr. Fang was at that moment perusing a leading article in a newspaper of the morning, adverting to some recent decision of his, and commending him, for the three hundred and fiftieth time, to the special and particular notice of the Secretary of State for the Home Department. He was out of temper; and he looked up with an angry scowl.

" 'Who are you?' said Mr. Fang.

"The old gentleman pointed with some surprise to his card. * * *

" 'Officer!' said Mr. Fang, throwing the paper on one side, 'What's this fellow charged with?'

" 'He's not charged at all, your worship," replied the officer.

" 'He appears against the boy, your worship.'

"His worship knew this perfectly well; but it was a good annoyance, and a safe one."

No evidence to support the charge against Oliver was presented but he was committed nevertheless to imprisonment for a period of three months. Mr. Brownlow finally secured Oliver's discharge however, and justice triumphed notwithstanding. This legal bully was evidently modeled after a notorious barrister of Dickens' time who occupied the office of Police Magistrate. As a result of the author's description of Magistrate Fang's treatment of Oliver, the real offender was removed from office by the Home Secretary. Here is first hand proof that the pen of Dickens was actually responsible for improvement in the judiciary.

In this same book we find a remark attributed to Bumble, the parish beadle, who named the foundlings in alphabetical order, probably quoted more frequently than even any part of the celebrated case of Bardell against Pickwick. Bumble and his wife were charged with selling certain articles left in the work house by

Oliver's mother.   The beadle attempted to excuse himself by saying:

"It was all Mrs. Bumble. She *would* do it."

"That is no excuse," replied Mr. Brownlow. "You were present on the occasion of the destruction of these trinkets, and, indeed, are the more guilty of the two, in the eye of the law; for the law supposes that your wife acts under your direction."

"If the law supposes that," said Mr. Bumble, squeezing his hat emphatically in both hands, "the law is a ass—a idiot. If that's the eye of the law, the law's a bachelor; and the worst I wish the law is, that his eye may be opened by experience—by experience."

Many other lawyers are introduced by Dickens. Eugene Rayburn of Our Mutual Friend, a briefless attorney, who hates his profession. Gloomy, indolent and unambitious, he is finally aroused from his lethargy by a fortunate marriage to a fine young woman. Mr. Henry Spiker, so cold a man that his head, instead of being grey, seemed to be sprinkled with hoar frost; and Mr. Tangle of Bleak House, a lawyer who knew more about the case of Jarndyce versus Jarndyce than any other person, and who was supposed not to have ever read anything else since he left school.

In the Battle of Life the firm of Snitchey and Craggs, country solicitors are important figures.

"Snitchey and Craggs had a snug little office on the old battle-ground, where they drove a snug little business, and fought a great many small pitched battles for a great many contending parties. Though it could hardly be said of these conflicts that they were running fights,—for in truth they generally proceeded at a snail's pace,—the part the Firm had in them came so far within the general denomination, that now they took at shot at this Plaintiff, and now aimed a chop at that Defendant, now made a heavy charge at an estate in Chancery, and now had some light skirmishing among an irregular body of small debtors, just as the occasion served, and the enemy happened to present himself. The Gazette was an important and profitable feature in some of their fields, as in fields of greater renown; and in most of the Actions wherein they showed their generalship, it was afterwards observed by the combatants that they had had great difficulty in making each other out, or in knowing with any degree of distinctness what they were about, in consequence of the vast amount of smoke by which they were surrounded."

In the Mystery of Edwin Drood, unfinished at the author's death, we meet Hiram Grewgious, the queer, shrewd old lawyer and his clerk Bazzard, who possessed a strange power over him.

There is Samuel Briggs "a mere machine, a sort of self-acting legal walking stick," Mr. Tipps, Mr. Fips, Mortimer Lightwood, and Mr. Rugg, a London solicitor with little practice, "a professional gentleman in an extremely small way." Their names alone create a mental picture in the mind of the reader. In fact, the genius of Dickens was nowhere displayed to greater advantage than in the names which he assigned to his characters.

"We in our profession are little else than mirrors after all, Mr. Alfred, but we are generally consulted by angry and quarrelsome people, who are not in their best looks, and it's rather hard to quarrel with us if we reflect unpleasant aspects."

Are these solicitors and barristers as presented by Dickens exaggerated types not found in real life? Perhaps their deficiencies are too numerous to create a complete illusion. However, it was a keen observer who sketched these men of the law and they fairly live as you read the fascinating tales in which they make their appearance. The weaknesses of the legal fraternity could not have been more effectively and graphically portrayed. The same type of pettifoggers as Dodson and Fogg still hatch their injudicious plots in law offices —the same kind of legal bully as Serjeant Buzfuz still attempts to mislead juries in courtrooms with occasional success. It is to be regretted that Dickens did not have more to say about the ethical lawyers, whose work is constructive and valuable to the communities where they reside. But perhaps they need no commendation on the theory that virtue is its own reward.

"It is night in Lincoln's Inn,—perplexed and troublous valley of the shadow of the law, where suitors generally find but little day,—and fat candles are snuffed out in offices, and clerks have rattled down the crazy wooden stairs, and dispersed. The bell that rings at nine o'clock has ceased its doleful clangour about nothing; the gates are shut; and the night-porter, a solemn warder with a mighty power of sleep, keeps guard in his lodge. From tiers of staircase windows, clogged lamps like the eyes of Equity, bleared Argus with a fathomless pocket for every eye and an eye upon

it, dimly blink at the stars. In dirty upper case-
ments, here and there, hazy little patches of candle-
light reveal where some wise draughtsman and
conveyancer yet toils for the entanglement of real
estate in meshes of sheepskin, in the average ratio
of about a dozen of sheep to an acre of land. Over
which bee like industry, these benefactors of their
species linger yet, though office hours be past, that
they may give, for every day, some good account
at last."—Bleak House.

www.ingramcontent.com/pod-product-compliance
Lightning Source LLC
Chambersburg PA
CBHW031417180326
41458CB00002B/415